ONE BIG HAPPY
ALL THE DIRT!

Rick Detorie

ONE BIG HAPPY
ALL THE DIRT!

Rick Detorie

NANTIER · BEALL · MINOUSTCHINE
Publishing inc.
new york

ISBN 1-56163-280-5
©2001 Creators Syndicate
Printed in Canada

The Story of "One Big Happy"
And all the dirt!

Rick Detorie started drawing cartoons as a child. At the age of 4, he won third prize for drawing a television set in a contest sponsored by Junket Gelatin. The prize was a transistor radio.

Actually, my mom had drawn it for me. To this day, she refuses to talk about it.

After receiving a BFA from Maryland Institute, College of Art, Rick Detorie moved to Los Angeles and got a job with an ad agency. He worked his way up from production artist to art director to creative director.

Hardly anyone in advertising wanted to be there. One copywriter was working on a novel, and another one was unsuccessfully sending out screenplays, waiting for his big break. The senior art director was developing a porn magazine. I was selling cartoons to magazines like Saturday Evening Post *and* Saturday Review.

With his freelance cartoon assignments mounting up, Rick Detorie quit the ad agency and devoted his attention full-time to cartooning. In addition to selling gag cartoons to magazines, he wrote and illustrated humor books, about 25 in total, commencing with *The Official Cat Dictionary*, and culminating with *How to Survive an Italian Family*. Somewhere along the way, he also hooked up with Bagdasarian Productions, proud owners of "Alvin and the Chipmunks," and drew Alvin and his brothers, Simon and Theodore, for record jackets and scores of merchandising products.

The year was 1987, and Rick Detorie decided that it was time for him to do a comic strip.

I'd always been a fan of comic strips, in particular, "Peanuts," and the then-new "Calvin and Hobbes." Besides, as a freelancer with varied and numerous income sources, my billing and payment schedules were always in a flux. With a nationally syndicated comic strip, I might actually begin to receive a regular paycheck, and a daily comic strip would mean steady work.

The thought did cross my mind, "What if I run out of ideas?" After all, in just one

Ruthie and Joe (then named Frankie) in their first incarnation. I switched to "Joe" because there are fewer letters in the name.

year, I'd have to come up with 365 funny ideas. Wouldn't the pressure be awesome? On the other hand, I only had to come up with one cartoon per day. That wasn't so difficult. If I managed to do two cartoons in one day, I could take a day off. That seemed like a pretty good deal. By taking it one day at a time, I could avoid thinking about the thousands of cartoons I'd have to produce over the next several years.

The first step in developing a comic strip was deciding the kind of strip it would be. Would it be political in nature? How about talking animals? Kids? The workplace? How about a politically savvy strip about talking animals in a child-oriented workplace, say a daycare center? What would please *everybody*?

He settled on a family strip.

My last book was How to Survive an Italian Family. *I decided to use that book as a jumping-off point to the strip. I would depict a traditional family (kids, parents, grandparents) in a realistic, slightly unconventional, and edgy manner. There would be no talking animals, no unbelievable situations, and no schmaltz. The strip would be a microcosm of family life, the day-to-day triumphs and tragedies in a household with young children who had easy access to their grandparents. It helped that my sisters and I had grown up right next door to our own grandparents.*

In developing the major characters, Rick Detorie decided on a happily married mom and dad, two children (a boy and a girl),

and two sets of grandparents.

Later, remembering a comic strip editor's advice to keep it simple and to focus on one central character, he eliminated two of the grandparents and zeroed in on the little daughter, Ruthie.

There were already a couple of blond-haired little boys on the comics pages: "Dennis the Menace," and Calvin of "Calvin and Hobbes," so this strip would be about a little dark-haired girl.

He decided to call it "One Big Happy."

I didn't like the name, but all the good titles with the word "family" in them were being used by TV shows, like "Family Ties" and "Family Matters," so I chose a title in which family was implied. I figured that once I got the strip accepted by a syndicate, the creative minds there would suggest a clever, catchier title.

I was wrong.

He set the strip in an unnamed, moderately sized city.

It's a whole lot like Baltimore.

When designing the characters, he patterned the grandfather after his own grandfather, Nick, and a friend's dad. Rose he refashioned from a grandmother character in his *How to Survive an Italian Family* book. The parents, Frank and Ellen, were lifted from an earlier comic strip he had developed and abandoned, and Joe was a newly designed character. Ruthie was a composite of Rick Detorie's two younger sisters. She looked like his little sister Sandy, and behaved like middle sister Terry.

Actually, Ruthie's stubbornness, curiosity, and defiance come from Terry. Ruthie's manipulative ways, rage against injustice and rudeness, and confusion over the English language come from me. Her other characteristics come from a variety of sources, none I'm willing to divulge.

As a practical guide to drawing the characters, he developed a model sheet for each of them. He drew each character's face and body from various angles, and referred to those sketches every time he drew the strip.

Hey, I know I don't draw all that well. I consider it a success if I draw something and someone else – without my help – can tell what it's supposed to be. Besides my problems with perspective, and those complex, hard-to-draw

A portion of Ruthie's model sheet

items like bicycles, cats, cars, dogs, silverware, and human hands (using a pair of scissors...yeesh!), my biggest challenge was making a character look recognizable from one panel to the next. Except for my experience with the Chipmunks, I'd never had to draw the same characters over and over again. So, early on I relied on my model sheets.

After sketching out about 50 daily strips and four Sundays, he selected 24 dailies and two Sundays for final inking. Next, he made copies of the finished work, assembled them in plastic report folders, and mailed them (each with a cover letter and a self-addressed stamped envelope) to the top seven newspaper syndicates that carried comic strips. He then sat back and waited for the syndicates to jump at the chance to launch this hot new property.

Yeah, right.

I already knew from my experience hawking cartoons to magazines that I should expect rejection. Based on the yearly submission rates of new comic strips to newspaper syndicates, the odds of one of them picking up "One Big Happy" were about 5,000 to 1.

I was prepared for the worst. While waiting for the rejection letters to come in, I was already developing my second comic strip, "Zerbyville," *the humorous adventures of a divorced mother of two moving her brood from a large city to a small town to work for the local newspaper. Also waiting in the wings was "Because I Said So!" a twisted look at those annoying things parents say, and a fourth (unnamed) strip about a bunch of talking animals and a Las Vegas showgirl stranded on a deserted island with nothing but satellite TV.*

I was determined to get something syndicated.

Within a couple of months of the initial mailing, the syndicates began returning "One Big Happy" with the standard rejection letter. Undaunted, he sent his second strip, "Zerbyville," to the syndicates, and as that strip was being rejected, he mailed out "Because I Said So!"

My plan was to bombard them with Rick Detorie comic strips until somebody sat up and took notice.

One day, at Creators Syndicate, President Rick Newcombe was leafing through "Because I Said So!" and said to the submissions editor, "Isn't this by that same guy who did that family strip? Whatever happened to that one? I liked that strip."

This was months after "One Big Happy" had received its final rejection from the last syndicate.

The four original grandparents: Rose, Nick, Faye and Bert

Sadly, it had long since been filed away in the dead comic strip drawer.

Rick Newcombe phoned Rick Detorie, and asked to see another sixty dailies of "One Big Happy."

After I hung up the phone, I did a fierce little dance around the kitchen.

Rick Detorie was happy to oblige, and within a month he signed a contract and was hard at work readying Ruthie, Grandpa, and the rest for the launch of "One Big Happy" on Sept. 11, 1988.

The next twenty pages contain some of the very first "One Big Happy" strips from 1988. Yes, the characters look different than they do today. That's because they have evolved. They don't age; they evolve.

We should all be so lucky.

15

16

22

23

JOE, I'M GOING CAMPING WITH MELISSA AND HER FAMILY, AND YOU'RE NOT!

OH, YEAH?

OH, YEAH...

WELL, RUTHIE, I'M GLAD I'M NOT GOING, BECAUSE CAMPING IS WAY TOO SCARY FOR ME!

HUH?!

LIKE, WHAT IF MELISSA'S FAMILY FORGETS YOU'RE WITH THEM, AND LEAVES YOU ALL ALONE IN THE WOODS?

OR, WHAT IF YOU'RE BITTEN BY AN EVIL BAT, AND TURNED INTO A ZOMBIE BAT SLAVE?

HURRY UP, WILL YA? I AIN'T GOT ALL NIGHT!

YES, MASTER.

OR, WHAT IF BIGFOOT COMES ALONG, SEES YOU IN YOUR SLEEPING BAG, AND THINKS YOU'RE A GIANT BURRITO?

YUM!

MOM!

WHAT DO YOU MEAN, YOU DON'T WANT TO GO CAMPING WITH MELISSA'S FAMILY?!

THAT'S RIGHT, AND THEY'RE TERRIBLE PEOPLE FOR EVEN ASKING ME!

24

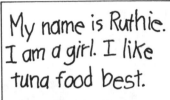

MOM, LOOK WHAT RUTHIE DID!

I GOT WATER IN MY EARS! I CAN'T HEAR ANYTHING!
YOU'LL SURVIVE.

WHAT?! WHAT'S ALIVE?!
GO PUT ON YOUR P.J.s, PLEASE.

WHAT?! I CAN STAY UP UNTIL TEN?!
NOW YOU'RE BEING SILLY, RUTHIE.

THANKS, MOM! MAKE MINE CHOCOLATE CHIP!

DADDY, WHAT DO YOU LOVE ABOUT MOMMY?
AHH... WHERE SHOULD I BEGIN?!

I LOVE THE WAY SHE BRUSHES HER HAIR. I LOVE THE WAY SHE SAYS INSURANCE. I LOVE HER WALK, ESPECIALLY FROM THE BACK! SHE LOOKS GREAT LEAVING THE ROOM!

I LOVE HER LAUGH, HER LIPS, AND HER ICED TEA, PLUS ABOUT A MILLION OTHER THINGS, RUTHIE.

DADDY LOVES IT WHEN YOU LEAVE THE ROOM.

We now fast-forward eight years...

ONE BIG HAPPY
RICK DETORIE

Children are from Pluto. Parents are from the moon.

WHEN THEY SAY:
I DON'T LIKE THIS STUFF!

WHAT THEY MEAN IS:
I JUST FINISHED OFF A HUGE BOX OF OREOS, AND I WON'T BE HUNGRY AGAIN UNTIL SOMETIME AFTER MIDNIGHT.

WHEN THEY SAY:
WE DON'T USE THAT KIND OF LANGUAGE AROUND HERE.

WHAT THEY MEAN IS:
WE DON'T USE THAT KIND OF LANGUAGE OUT LOUD OR IN YOUR PRESENCE.

WHEN THEY SAY:
IT'S NOT FAIR!

WHAT THEY MEAN IS:
I'M NOT GETTING **MY** WAY!

WHEN THEY SAY:
IT'S A LOVELY DAY! WHY DON'T YOU PLAY OUTSIDE?

WHAT THEY MEAN IS:
GET OUT OF HERE!

WHEN THEY SAY:
COME GIVE ME A HUG!

WHAT THEY MEAN IS:
LET ME SEE IF YOU WASHED YOUR EARS.

WHEN THEY SAY:
DAD, WILL YOU HELP ME WITH MY HOMEWORK?

WHAT THEY MEAN IS:
DAD, WILL YOU DO MY HOMEWORK FOR ME?

WHEN THEY SAY:
MAYBE ALISSA'S MOM WANTS HER **HOME** FOR DINNER.

WHAT THEY MEAN IS:
I WANT THIS DESPICABLE LITTLE BRAT OUT OF MY HOUSE **NOW**!

WHEN THEY SAY:
I **HEARD** YOU, MOM! I'M TURNING IT OFF NOW.

WHAT THEY MEAN IS:
I'LL WATCH UNTIL A COMMERCIAL, THEN I'LL FLIP THROUGH ABOUT SIXTY MORE CHANNELS BEFORE I TURN IT OFF.

WHEN THEY SAY:
I'M NOT GOING TO TELL YOU AGAIN!

WHAT THEY MEAN IS:
I'M GOING TO TELL YOU TWENTY-FOUR MORE TIMES UNTIL YOU FINALLY DO IT.

31

33

SCHOOL IS A VERY WEIRD PLACE WITH LOTS OF STRANGE RULES.

GROWN-UPS MAKE UP A LOT OF THIS STUFF JUST TO TORTURE US KIDS.

I MEAN, MOST OF IT IS SO CRAZY, IT'S A WONDER ANYBODY BELIEVES IT AT ALL!

LIKE WHAT?

DID YOU KNOW THAT THERE'S AN "S" IN "ISLAND"?!

NO!

5. Name an animal that lives in the forest.

The skunk

6. Name another animal that lives in the forest.

The skunk's wife

DO YOU THINK MY MOM WOULD ENJOY *MAVERICK*?

OH, YES... SHE THINKS JAMES GARNER IS SEXY.

VIDEO RENTALS

SEXY?! **MY MOM SAID THAT JAMES GARNER IS SEXY**?

WELL, WHAT SHE SAID WAS...

"HONEY, I'D LEAVE MY PORCH LIGHT ON FOR **HIM**!"

WOW.

THE WOMAN'S AN ANIMAL.

VIDEO RENTALS

YOU'RE NOT A BIG COUNTRY MUSIC FAN, ARE YOU, RUTHIE?

I AM TOO, GRANDPA!

COUNTRY MUSIC IS MY MOST FAVORITE MUSIC! I CAN SING ALMOST ALL THE WORDS!

I KNOW ALL ABOUT THE BIG COUNTRY STARS! I'M PRETTY MUCH AN EXPERT, YES I AM.

REALLY? WHO'S YOUR FAVORITE COUNTRY SINGER?

AMMONIA JUDD.

GOOD AFTERNOON, BOYS AND GIRLS, I'M MISS TINA!

HEY! WHERE'S OUR REGULAR LIBRARY LADY?!

STORY HOUR

FEAR NOT, YOUNG STORY FANS. I SHARE YOUR SENSE OF LOSS CONCERNING MY REPLACING MISS BETTY AS YOUR PRIMARY STORYTELLER.

STOR HOU

BUT, I ASSURE YOU, I'M VERY SENSITIVE TO YOUR NEEDS DURING THIS MOST DIFFICULT TRANSITION PERIOD.

NEVER MIND ALL THAT. MISS BETTY OWES ME A QUARTER!

RUTHIE, I HEAR THERE'S A NEW STORYTELLER AT THE LIBRARY.

YOU KNOW, GRANDPA, I DON'T LIKE CHANGE.

AH YES, CHANGE OFTEN MAKES FOR A DIFFICULT ADJUSTMENT. JUST WHEN YOU'RE STARTING TO GET USED TO SOMETHING, **BAM!** IT CHANGES.

BUT REMEMBER THAT ATTITUDE IS EVERYTHING. IF YOU GO IN BELIEVING THAT CHANGE WILL BE GOOD, IT OFTENTIMES IS.

NO, GRANDPA, I DON'T LIKE **CHANGE.**

I LIKE ONES AND FIVES— **FOLDING** MONEY, NOT CHANGE!

39

JUST TRY IT, RUTHIE. HOW DO YOU KNOW YOU DON'T LIKE IT IF YOU'VE NEVER TRIED IT?

YEAH, BUT WHAT IT WOULD'A BEEN **IS**, IF I WOULD'A HAD WHAT WOULD'A BEEN THIS, I WOULD'A LIKED IT AT ALL **NO WAY**, MOM!

THAT WAS A SENTENCE?

PART OF IT WAS, I THINK.

WHEW! PHIL AND DIANE ARE BICKERING AGAIN. I JUST GOT OFF THE PHONE WITH THEM, TRYING TO SORT THINGS OUT.

NOW I SHOULD CALL ANDREW TO REMIND HIM TO GO IN FOR A DENTAL CHECKUP.

ROSE, WHY MUST YOU INVOLVE YOURSELF IN EVERYONE'S BUSINESS?

BECAUSE I'M THEIR MOTHER, NICK. THEIR BUSINESS **IS** MY BUSINESS.

I SHOULD TAKE A BREATHER, THOUGH. I'M WORN OUT.

MEDDLE FATIGUE.

IT NEVER COMES WHEN I **NEED** IT.

IT'S TOTALLY NOT FAIR, AND IT MAKES ME FEEL VERY SAD, MOSTLY.

SOMETIMES IT CHOPS DOCTOR QUINN RIGHT IN HALF! IT COMES RIGHT IN THE MIDDLE.

AND TODAY'S GRIPE IS ABOUT...?

HER BEDTIME.

AND THE CLOTHES FIT FUNNY!

44

I NEED A FOUR-LETTER WORD FOR STANZA.

TONY.

YEAH, ISN'T THAT THE NAME OF THAT NICE KID IN THAT SITCOM ABOUT HOUSEKEEPING?

STANZA, NOT DANZA.

YES, THAT'S IT, TONY DANZA. *HOOVER'S BOSS*, OR SOMETHING LIKE THAT.

STANZA, LIKE IN A SONG!

ROSE, HONEY, I DON'T KNOW IF HE CAN SING.

"I MUST TELL MY BROTHER DUNCAN," SAID THE PRINCE.

DUNCAN?

THAT'S AN ODD NAME. I NEVER HEARD **THAT** NAME BEFORE!

OH, IT'S NOT SO ODD. I KNOW **LOTS** OF DUNCANS.

YOU DO NOT, RUTHIE!

DO TOO, JOE!

OKAY, NAME ONE!

DUNCAN DONUTS.

HERE, GRANDPA, TRY THIS! I PUT MY SECRET SAUCE ON IT!

MMM... **GOOD!** WHAT'S YOUR SECRET SAUCE?

KETCHUP?! WHAT MAKES THAT SECRET?

WHISPERING MAKES IT SECRET.

One Big Happy
Rick Detorie

"IT IS A BOY," SHE SAID. "YOU HAVE A SON."

HE GAZED UPON HIS WIFE AND SON WITH HAPPINESS AND PRIDE.

RUNNING DEER TOOK HIS NEWBORN SON OUTSIDE TO NAME HIM.

A SOARING EAGLE WAS THE FIRST THING HE SAW, AND THAT IS THE NAME HE GAVE TO HIS SON: SOARING EAGLE.

NEAT! I WISH I HAD A COOL NAME LIKE THAT.

YEAH, COOL!

WHY DIDN'T YOU NAME **ME** LIKE THAT, DAD?

TOO IMPRACTICAL, A DIFFERENT SITUATION AND CUSTOMS...

BUT WHAT IF YOU **WOULD'A** GIVEN ME A NAME LIKE THAT? WHAT WOULD MY NAME BE?

WHAT WAS THE FIRST THING YOU SAW AFTER I WAS BORN?

LET'S SEE...

YOUR NAME WOULD BE...

CRABBY HEAD NURSE.

OH!

I KIND OF LIKE IT.

NOT CHANNEL ELEVEN... I CAN'T STAND THAT GUY'S HAIR.

OH NO, NOT THAT CHARACTER ON FOUR. HE SAYS "IF YOU WILL" EVERY TEN SECONDS.

SNOW

THE COLD FRONT, IF YOU WILL, IS MOVING EAST...

NO, NOT HER! SHE LEFT HER HUSBAND AND KIDS TO RUN OFF WITH THE AFTERNOON SPORTS GUY.

CLICK

ROSE, HONEY, I JUST WANT TO FIND OUT ABOUT THE BLIZZARD.

LOOKING OUT THE WINDOW WOULD BE A LOT LESS AGGRAVATING.

HAPPY VALENTINE'S DAY, RUTHIE! YOU'RE MY ONE AND ONLY!

JAMES!

WOW, I'M ALL EMBARRASSED! I DIDN'T KNOW YOU FELT THIS WAY ABOUT ME! I MEAN, I NEVER...

JAMES?

HAPPY VALENTINE'S DAY, CAROL ANN! YOU'RE MY ONE AND ONLY!

OH, HOW CUTE!

HAPPY VALENTINE'S DAY, GRANDMA!

HOW THOUGHTFUL OF YOU TO GIVE ME A TINY BOX OF CHOCOLATES!

THAT'S BECAUSE YOU KNOW THAT I'M CUTTING BACK ON SWEETS, ISN'T THAT RIGHT, RUTHIE?

NO, THAT'S BECAUSE I DIDN'T WANT TO SPEND A LOT OF MONEY.

ONE BIG HAPPY

Rick Detorie

FOOD EATEN AT A COUNTER...

ON THE GROUND...

OR IN BED, TASTES BETTER THAN FOOD EATEN AT A TABLE.

ANY FOOD THAT COMES WITH A TOY PRIZE IS "GOOD EATIN'."

THE ONLY GOOD FISH COMES IN FROZEN STICKS.

KETCHUP CAN SAVE ANYTHING.

IF YOU CAN EAT IT WITH YOUR HANDS, IT'S GOOD FOOD.

IF THERE'S A PICTURE OF THE FOOD ON THE MENU, IT'S GONNA BE GOOD.

IF THERE'S A PICTURE OF THE FOOD ON THE WALL, IT'S GONNA BE GREAT.

IF THERE'S A PICTURE ON THE WALL, AND THE FOOD HAS A FUNNY NAME, IT'S MOST EXCELLENT.

89¢

CHEESY BOPPER BURGER

ALL GREEN FOOD TASTES LOUSY...

EXCEPT LIME JELLO.

FOOD YOU FIND LATER IN YOUR HAIR, MOUTH, OR CLOTHES, IS OKAY TO EAT (AS LONG AS IT DIDN'T TOUCH THE FLOOR).

IF YOU HAVE TO DRESS UP TO EAT, IT'S GONNA BE A BAD MEAL.

WARNING SIGNS:

I PUT ON HARD SHOES FOR THIS?!

CLOTH NAPKIN

YOUR NAME ON A LI'L CARD

GLASS ON A POLE

GEE, RUTHIE, HOW DO YOU KNOW SO MUCH ABOUT FOOD?

BECAUSE, JAMES, I'VE BEEN EATING IT JUST ABOUT MY WHOLE ENTIRE LIFE!

ONE BIG happy

RICK DETORIE

TODAY'S TOPIC IS PARENTS, AND WHAT A PAIN IN THE NECK THEY ARE... JOE?

THANK YOU, MISS BLUNT-AS-ALWAYS-RUTHIE. BUT SERIOUSLY, FOLKS, WE HAVE SOME QUESTIONS FOR YOU PARENT TYPES, QUESTIONS LIKE...

WHY DO YOU ALWAYS ANSWER QUESTIONS THE SAME BORING OLD WAY?

BECAUSE **EVERY** DAY IS CHILDREN'S DAY!

WHY DO YOU ALWAYS WANT US TO TELL THE TRUTH, EXCEPT SOMETIMES?

MOMMY, THAT MAN HAS A BIG BEHIND.

RUTHIE, SHUSH!

PARENTS! WHO CAN FIGURE THEM OUT?

WHY DO YOU TELL US TO PIPE DOWN, THEN WHEN WE **ARE** QUIET, YOU ACT LIKE SOMETHING IS WRONG?

WHAT'S GOING ON IN HERE?

WHY DO YOU ASK SILLY QUESTIONS?

WHERE'S MY CHANGE?

HUH?

PARENTS HAVE A WEIRD WAY OF TALKING!

BUT THIS MORNING YOU SAID WE COULD DO IT!

I **SAID** I WOULD **THINK** ABOUT IT.

BUT "THINK ABOUT IT" MEANS **YES!**

WHY DO YOU ALWAYS TAKE OUR PICTURE WHEN WE LOOK LIKE DWEEBS?

I MEAN, **REALLY!**

WHY DO YOU WORK SO HARD TO GET US TO TALK...

SAY "MAMA". SAY "MAMA", RUTHIE.!

BUT, MOM, I NEVER GET MY WAY! I HAVE NO RIGHTS!

UH-HUH, THAT'S NICE, DEAR.

UH-HUH!

WHY DO YOU MAKE IT SO THAT THE FOOD THAT'S **GOOD** FOR US TASTES SO **BAD?**

THEN, WHEN WE FINALLY **DO** TALK, YOU DON'T LISTEN TO US?

ALSO, PARENTS WALK TOO FAST OR TOO SLOW; MAKE US BE NICE TO PEOPLE WE DON'T LIKE; GET TOO CARRIED AWAY WITH NEATNESS; TALK ON THE PHONE TOO MUCH; BUY GENERIC...

60

WEDDING TIME! BARBIE AND G.I. JOE ARE GETTIN' MARRIED!

MARRIED?!

DON'T WORRY, GRANDMA. THEY'RE BOTH GROWN-UPS, AND THEY GRADUATED FROM COLLEGE, AND THEY HAVE CAREERS.

THEY ALREADY AGREED ON MONEY STUFF AND HOW TO RAISE THEIR KIDS, AND THEY DON'T MAKE EACH OTHER CRAZY.

OKAY, THEN.

GEE, GRANDMA, IT'S NOT EASY PLAYING DOLLS WITH YOU!

NO, DEAR, BUT ULTIMATELY, IT'S MORE REWARDING.

3. Jimmy has a problem. He has completed four spelling tests so far this month.

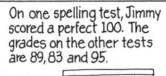

On one spelling test, Jimmy scored a perfect 100. The grades on the other tests are 89, 83 and 95.

Now Jimmy wants to figure out the average score of all four tests. How would you solve Jimmy's problem?

With a calculator.

HI, RUTHANN, JAMES!

HI, MISS AVIS. WE'RE PLAYIN' SCHOOL, AND NOW WE'RE ON A FIELD TRIP!

A FIELD TRIP?! HOW EXCITING! WHERE ARE YOU GOING TODAY ON YOUR FIELD TRIP?

TO A FIELD!

YOU KNOW ANY AROUND HERE?

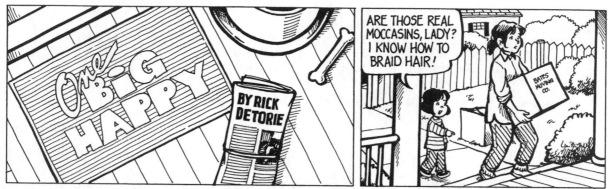

NO, I DID NOT CALL MY SISTER BARBARA.

BUT, ROSE, IT'S HER BIRTHDAY!

LISTEN, IF BARBARA WANTS TO TALK TO ME, **SHE** CAN CALL **ME**.

RING

HELLO?

IT'S BARBARA.

I'M NOT HERE.

SO AUNT BARBARA TURNED EIGHTY!

YEAH, BIG DEAL.

MA, ISN'T IT ABOUT TIME TO END THIS FEUD BETWEEN YOU TWO? AUNT BARBARA MADE THE FIRST MOVE BY CALLING YOU YESTERDAY.

HAH!

WELL, AT LEAST IT WAS A GESTURE!

OKAY, FINE. I'LL GIVE HER A GESTURE RIGHT BACK.

BUT NOT IN FRONT OF THE CHILDREN.

GEE, GRANDMA SURE HATES AUNT BARBARA!

AIN'T THAT THE TRUTH!

DOES THAT MEAN WE HAVE TO HATE AUNT BARBARA, TOO?

NO, RUTHIE, THEIR GRUDGE IS BETWEEN THE TWO OF THEM.

NO ONE, REGARDLESS OF HOW GUILTY THEY MIGHT TRY TO MAKE YOU FEEL, HAS THE RIGHT TO TELL YOU WHO TO LIKE OR DISLIKE.

OH.

SO, THEN, IT'S OKAY TO TELL GRANDMA THAT AUNT BARBARA IS NEXT DOOR AT OUR HOUSE?

NO!

WELL, AUNT BARBARA, MY MOM **IS** AT HOME.

JOE, YOU NEED A HAIRCUT!

I'M ALLERGIC TO CAT HAIR!

YOU CALL THIS CHAIR COMFORTABLE?

THESE NEW DENTURES ARE KILLING ME!

WHAT'S THAT HORRIBLE SMELL?

AND IS YOUR MOTHER COMING OVER TO SEE ME?

NO.

WELL, IT'S HER LOSS!

GRANDMA, WHY DON'T YOU LIKE AUNT BARBARA?

SHE'S A MEAN PERSON, RUTHIE, WHO'S NEVER BEEN NICE TO ME.

AND IF SOMEONE TREATS YOU BADLY, THERE'S NO REASON IN THE WORLD YOU SHOULD PRETEND YOU LIKE THAT PERSON.

UNLESS IT'S SOMEONE YOU **HAVE** TO BE CIVIL TO, LIKE YOUR BOSS OR YOUR TEACHER...

OR THE ICE CREAM MAN.

OR THE ICE CREAM MAN.

RUTHIE, I THOUGHT YOU WERE GOING TO HAVE DINNER AT YOUR GRANDMA'S!

I CHANGED MY MIND, MOM.

GRANDMA'S FIXIN' THAT WEIRD SQUISHY BALONEY STUFF I DON'T LIKE SO MUCH.

WEIRD SQUISHY BALONEY STUFF?

AH, BALONEY!

ABALONE.

YEAH, GROSS!

ONE BIG HAPPY

by Rick DeTorie

SUGAR AND SPICE AND EVERYTHING NICE, THAT'S WHAT LITTLE GIRLS ARE MADE OF.

WHAT LITTLE GIRLS ARE *REALLY* MADE OF

by Joe (the truly great one)

YEAH, RIGHT!

Whinies and tattles,

I'M TELLIN' ON YOU!

Boo-hoos and battles,

SOB!

Fish sticks jammed in with a glove.

RUTHIE!

Bossin' and fussin',

DO IT NOW!

Ramblin' and cussin',

THEN, UM... OH, ∅☆#!!!

Mustard that shoots from above.

RUTHIE!

Nasties and pouties,

Innies and outies,

That's what little girls are made of.

I JUST WANTED TO SET THE RECORD STRAIGHT.

MISTER, I DON'T LIKE THE COMIC BOOKS YOU HAVE IN THIS STORE.

THERE AREN'T ENOUGH **FUNNY** COMICS! THEY'RE MOSTLY SCARY STORIES WITH BIG WORDS ABOUT THESE MUSCLE PEOPLE DOING NASTY THINGS TO EACH OTHER!

YEAH, WELL, I GUESS IT ALL DEPENDS ON WHERE YOU'RE COMING FROM.

I'M COMING FROM DOWN HERE!

GRANDPA, I HAVE A GUARDIAN ANGEL!

UH-HUH... WHAT'S YOUR ANGEL'S NAME?

TEX.

HE TOLD YOU THAT?

HE DIDN'T HAVE TO. THE BOOTS AND HAT ARE A DEAD GIVEAWAY.

DO YOU KNOW WHAT VEGETABLE I LIKE, MOM? THAT DOODGER VEGETABLE!

DOODGER VEGETABLE?

YEAH, I HAD IT AT THAT RESTAURANT LAST WEEK. REMEMBER?

THE VEGETABLE DU JOUR?

YEAH, IT WAS YELLOW. YELLOW DOODGER VEGETABLE.

"I AM SO TIRED," SAID THE SHOEMAKER, "I CANNOT WAIT ANY LONGER."

"OH, JUST WAIT FOR ANOTHER COUPLE OF MINUTES," WHISPERED HIS WIFE.

AT THE LAST STROKE OF MIDNIGHT, A GROUP OF TINY ELVES ENTERED THE ROOM AND SCAMPERED TO THE WORK TABLE.

THE SHOEMAKER AND HIS WIFE WATCHED FROM BEHIND THE DOOR AS THE BROWNIES HAMMERED AND SEWED, MAKING A NEW PAIR OF SHOES.

"GOLLY," SAID THE SHOEMAKER, "I HAD OFTEN HEARD THAT BROWNIES COME TO HELP THOSE WHO NEED IT"...

"BUT I HAD NO IDEA THAT IT WAS THEY WHO WERE WORKING FOR US."

"NOR I," SAID HIS WIFE, "BUT LOOK, THE POOR LITTLE THINGS DON'T HAVE ANY CLOTHES. I SHOULD THINK THEY'D BE COLD THESE CHILLY NIGHTS."

"I'LL MAKE THEM SOME CLOTHES," SHE WHISPERED, "PANTS AND SHIRTS AND COATS."

"GOOD IDEA," SAID THE SHOEMAKER, "AND I'LL MAKE THEM SOME SHOES!"

ANY GOOD STORIES TODAY, RUTHIE?

NOT REALLY... JUST ONE ABOUT SOME NAKED GIRL SCOUTS BREAKIN' INTO A HOUSE.

JOE, WHY DO YOU HANG AROUND WITH THAT TREVOR? HE'S NOT A VERY NICE BOY.

YEAH, I KNOW, GRANDPA, BUT TREVOR KNOWS JESSIE GARCIA AND TODD LUTZ!

JESSIE IS, LIKE, MISSING A TOE; AND WHEN TODD DRINKS CHOCOLATE MILK, HE CAN SQUIRT IT BACK OUT HIS NOSE.'

OH... SO TREVOR IS SOCIALLY CONNECTED.

BIG TIME!

YOU'LL HAVE A GLASS OF MILK...

NO, MOM, I WANT A SODA! PLE-E-E-ZE?

ALL RIGHT, RUTHIE, IF YOU CAN SIT DOWN AND BEHAVE YOURSELF, I'LL LET YOU GET A SODA.

NEVER MIND, I'LL JUST HAVE THE MILK, THEN.

A GIRL IN MY CLASS NAMED STACEY IS STUCK UP!

REALLY?

RUTHIE, DO YOU KNOW WHAT "STUCK UP" MEANS?

SURE, GRANDPA, IT MEANS SHE WAS ROBBED!

NO, NO, NO. YOU'RE THINKING OF "HELD UP." "STUCK UP" MEANS SHE'S RATHER SNOTTY.

WELL, SHE **HAS** HAD HER SHARE OF COLDS LATELY.

MOM, WHAT'S ASTROLOGY?

IT'S SORT OF A SCIENCE.

NO, IT'S MORE OF A BELIEF, REALLY, THAT THE POSITIONS OF THE SUN AND STARS AND PLANETS AFFECT HUMAN AFFAIRS AND CAN FORETELL THE FUTURE.

SO, FOR EXAMPLE, IF VENUS AND SATURN ARE ALIGNED JUST SO, ON TUESDAY, YOU MIGHT FIND A COUPLE OF BUCKS IN THE SOFA CUSHIONS.

OH.

AND A **GROWN-UP** THOUGHT THIS UP?

YES, BUT DON'T HOLD THAT AGAINST **ALL** OF US.

SOMETIMES A MAMA BIRD WILL ACTUALLY PUSH A BABY BIRD OUT OF THE NEST.

IT'S TOTALLY DEAD.

BUT **WHY**, GRANDMA?

MAYBE THE NEST IS TOO CROWDED, OR THE BABY BIRD IS DAMAGED OR ILL.

WELL, COULDN'T THE BABY BIRD GO LIVE SOMEPLACE ELSE, LIKE THE GRANDMA BIRD'S NEST?

MAYBE THE GRANDMA BIRD DOESN'T HAVE HER OWN NEST! MAYBE SHE LIVES IN A RETIREMENT NEST!

NATURE IS SO **RUDE**!

WOE IS ME! CLANG, CLANG! TOOT!

WHAT'S GOING ON?

WE FOUND A DEAD BABY BIRD, AND NOW WE'RE GOING TO BURY HIM.

WOE, OH, WOE!

CLANG!

YEAH, HIS LIFE WASN'T SO GREAT, BUT HIS DEATH IS GONNA BE SOME BIG DEAL!

LET'S SEE... WHICH STORY WOULD YOU LIKE TO HEAR?

I KNOW!

HOW ABOUT THAT THING YOU READ TO GRANDPA?!

THING?

HE SAID YOU READ IT TO HIM THIS MORNING. MAYBE IT'S STILL HERE!

WHAT ARE YOU LOOKING FOR?

THE RIOT ACT!

YOU SELL DRAWINGS?

GOOD ART BY RUTHIE

UH-HUH.

Only 5¢ Drawed while you wait!

I DIDN'T WANT TO AT FIRST, BUT MY GRANDPA SAYS IT'S GOOD 'SPERIENCE FOR ME TO DEAL WITH THE PUBLIC.

UH... ARE YOU THE PUBLIC?

YEAH, I GUESS I AM.

Only 5¢ Drawed while you wait!

PROUD TO KNOW YA, HON!

Only 5¢ wed while ou wait!

"GAZING UPON THE FIERY DESTRUCTION OF SODOM, LOT'S WIFE TURNED INTO A PILLAR OF SALT."

WHOA!

BIBLE STORIES

BUT I GUESS THAT'S WHAT HAPPENS WHEN YOU DON'T PAY ATTENTION TO WHERE YOU'RE GOING.'

YOU WRECK THE CAR.'

THE CAR?!

YEAH, SHE PROBABLY MEANT TO TURN INTO A PARKING LOT.'

GRANDPA, IS IT POLITE TO ASK SOMEBODY WHAT THEIR GRADES ARE?

HMM...

NO, PROBABLY NOT, RUTHIE.

BUT THEN HOW WILL I KNOW IF THE GUY I MARRY IS A BIG DUMMY?!

OH, YOUR GRANDMA WILL BE MORE THAN HAPPY TO TELL YOU THAT!

I CAPTURED HER, MASTER!

GOOD! NOW LET'S BRAINWASH HER!

BRAINWASH?!! NO! NO! NO!

GEE, RUTHIE, CHILL OUT, WILL YA!

ARE YOU GONNA GET MY HAIR WET?!

NO.

OKAY, THEN!

YOU DIDN'T STUDY FOR THIS SPELLING TEST, DID YOU, JOE?

I DID TO, DAD!

WHAT'S THIS WORD SUPPOSED TO BE?

PRESHATE!

USE IT IN A SENTENCE.

I PRESHATE YOU NOT MAKIN' FUN OF MY SPELLING!

JOE...

I'LL BE ERICA, THE GLAMOROUS RICH GIRL, AND YOU'RE DIMITRI, MY RICH BOYFRIEND.

BOYFRIEND?!

OH, DIMITRI, DAHLING, YOU LOVE ME SO MUCH YOU MAY KISS MY HAND! WATCH OUT FOR MY JEWELS.

LOVE YOU?

LOVE? WHAT IS LOVE, YOU ASK? DIMITRI, YOU SILLY BOY, YOU WILL KNOW WHEN IT'S LOVE! LOVE HITS YOU LIKE A...

BOINK!

HEY, BE CAREFUL!

WATCH WHERE YOU THROW THAT BALL!

YOU BIG KIDS DON'T OWN THIS PARK!

AH, PIPE DOWN, YA SQUIRT! HOWS ABOUT I SWAT YOU DOWN LIKE A PESKY LI'L MOSQUITO, HUH?

HEY! YOU LAY A FINGER ON THAT CHILD, AND I'LL PUT YOU IN THE HOSPITAL.

UH...

I DIDN'T KNOW YOUR GRANDADDY'S A DOCTOR!

IT'S NEWS TO ME!

JOE, WHAT'S WITH RUTHIE?

SHH... NOT SO LOUD, GRANDPA! WE'RE ALMOST AT THE PARK.

THE BIG KIDS AT THE PARK GOT MAD AT HER YESTERDAY, SO TODAY, SHE'S NOT RUTHIE.

SHE'S LATASHA, OKAY?

ONE BIG HAPPY

GRANDMA, GUESS WHAT I'VE BEEN DOING?!

YOU'VE BEEN HELPING YOUR DADDY SET UP THE BARBECUE GRILL.

YES! CHARCOAL IS FUN!

WASH YOUR HANDS, PLEASE.

WHAT ARE YOU FIXIN', GRANDMA?

CHICKEN FOR THE BARBECUE.

OH.

OH MY GOODNESS!

WHAT IS IT, RUTHIE?

CHICKEN?! DO YOU MEAN THAT **THAT'S** THE SAME ANIMAL THAT USED TO HAVE FEATHERS?!

WELL... CERTAINLY.

THE SAME BIRD THAT USED TO RUN AROUND A FARM AND LAY EGGS AND HAVE BABY CHICKS IS NOW ALL DEAD AND NAKED AND CHOPPED UP, AND WE'RE SUPPOSED TO **EAT** IT? **GROSS!**

FORGET IT! NO CHICKEN FOR ME, NOT EVER!

I'LL HAVE A HOT DOG INSTEAD.

OH MY GOODNESS!

RUTHIE, I DON'T WANT YOU GETTING ANYTHING ON THIS FLOOR. UNDERSTAND?

YES, MOM.

ELLEN!

MOTHER! WHAT ARE YOU DOING HERE?

GRANDMA MYRNA!

OH, I'M IN PAIN, BABY. THE MOST TERRIBLE THING HAS HAPPENED!

I'M GETTING A DIVORCE!

ANOTHER ONE?

WELL, DON'T GET IT ON THIS FLOOR!

MOTHER, WHY ARE YOU AND RAY GETTING A DIVORCE?

OH... THE USUAL REASONS.

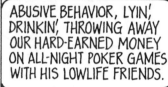

ABUSIVE BEHAVIOR, LYIN', DRINKIN', THROWING AWAY OUR HARD-EARNED MONEY ON ALL-NIGHT POKER GAMES WITH HIS LOWLIFE FRIENDS.

HE DID ALL THAT?

NO, I DID, AND HE GOT SICK AND TIRED OF IT.

MOTHER, THIS IS YOUR FIFTH DIVORCE! YOU'VE GOT TO STOP MARRYING EVERY MAN WHO HAPPENS ALONG.

ELLEN, I LOVED EVERY ONE OF MY HUSBANDS.

YOU COULDN'T HAVE **LOVED** THEM, MOM. YOU BARELY **KNEW** THEM!

NOT TRUE! NOW, TAKE YOUR DADDY. I KNEW TRENT BETTER THAN ANY WOMAN COULD KNOW A MAN!

MY FATHER WAS HARVEY.

AND I WAS PRETTY FAMILIAR WITH **HIM**, TOO.

GRANDPA, GRANDMA MYRNA IS GETTING A DIVORCE.

A DIVORCE?!

YES, IT'S THIS AWFUL THING THAT HAPPENS TO GROWN-UPS. FIRST YOU START TO FEEL BAD ALL OVER...

AND YOUR EYES GET ALL RED AND YOUR NOSE RUNS, THEN YOU START TO SEE THINGS!

REALLY?

YES, THE FIRST THING GRANDMA MYRNA SAW WAS A LAWYER.

THIS IS THE WAY TO LIVE!

I BEG YOUR PARDON?

BACK TO REALITY... AWAY FROM THE COMPLICATIONS AND DISTRACTIONS OF THE BIG CITY!

THIS IS THE REAL ME, BACK TO NATURE! ENJOYING THE SIMPLE PLEASURES!

BY THE WAY, DO YOU KNOW OF ANYPLACE CLOSE BY WHERE I CAN GET MY EYELASHES DYED?

LOOK, MOM, WE HAD OUR NAILS DONE!

YES, AND I PROMISED RUTHIE THAT IF SHE STOPPED BITING HER FINGERNAILS FOR A WHOLE WEEK, I'D BUY HER A...A...

A FUN FACTORY COOKIE MAKER!

YEAH, THAT'S IT.

BUT RUTHIE DOESN'T BITE...

MOM!

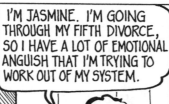

94

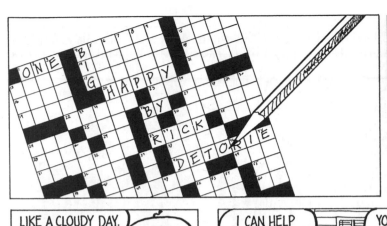

99

I HAVE TO GO TO THE BATHROOM.

I DON'T LIKE NO STORIES 'LESS THEY GOTS SHOOTIN' AND FIGHTIN'!

Library STORY HOUR

HUSH UP, JAMES! NO MATTER HOW BAD SHE TELLS THE STORY, YOU'LL LISTEN TO IT AND YOU'LL ENJOY IT.

NO, I WON'T!

SURE YOU WILL, 'CUZ IF YOU DON'T ENJOY IT, YOU'LL FEEL BAD AND SUFFER A LOT.

HOW DO **YOU** KNOW?

'CUZ I'LL MAKE SURE OF THAT.

I'M ENJOYING! **I'M ENJOYING!**

HOW DO YOU KNOW WHEN ART IS **GOOD** ART, RUTHIE?

GOOD ART IS WHEN YOU STAY IN THE LINES.

UNLESS YOU'RE MAKIN' ART WITH **NO** LINES, OR YOU'RE NOT **SUPPOSED** TO STAY IN 'EM!

AND SOME ART IS UGLY, BUT AS LONG AS IT DOESN'T GIVE YOU A HEADACHE, IT CAN STILL BE GOOD ART.

SO ART IS IN THE EYE OF THE BEHOLDER?

OR IN YOUR NOSE OR ON YOUR PANTS, DEPENDING WHERE IT SPLASHES.

THE GIANT SEA SLUG RISES OUT OF THE WATER.

HUNGRY, IT SEARCHES FOR FOOD, LEAVING A SLIMY PATH OF DESTRUCTION IN ITS WAKE.

HUMONGOUS, IT IS THE MOST DISGUSTING CREATURE IN THE UNIVERSE, YET IT SEEMS QUITE PROUD OF ITS GROSSNESS.

URRRP!

WHAT ARE **YOU** LOOKIN' AT, KID?

UH... NICE SPEEDO, MISTER.

HI, FRANK! RENTING FOUR VIDEOS TODAY, HUH?

YES, ALL BY POPULAR DEMAND.

LET'S SEE... *THE MUPPET ADVENTURE, EL DORADO, HOW TO BEAT THE ODDS IN VEGAS* AND *SEW MANY QUILTS.*

AH! I SEE ONE THAT YOUR MOTHER REQUESTED.

ONE?

SHE REQUESTED **ALL** OF THEM!

TO BECOME A CHAMPION TAKES HARD WORK AND DETERMINATION.

INTENSE TRAINING IS ESSENTIAL. NO PAIN, NO GAIN.'

AND A DEDICATED PERSONAL TRAINER SUCH AS YOURSELF IS AN INVALUABLE ASSET!

ALL RIGHT, LET THE GAMES BEGIN!

G... 52.!

DAD, YOU'RE NOT A VERY RESPONSIBLE PARENT!

NOBODY'S PERFECT, JOE.

I MEAN IT! HE'S DEAD, AND IT'S **YOUR** FAULT!

I'M A HEARTLESS SCOUNDREL!

JUST AN INNOCENT LI'L CLICK BEETLE, MINDING HIS OWN BUSINESS...

IN THE PRIME OF HIS LIFE!

YOU'RE SUPPOSED TO **CHECK** KIDS' POCKETS BEFORE YOU DO LAUNDRY!

I'M A MURDERER!

JAMES, THERE'S A LOLLIPOP IN YOUR HAIR!

SO THAT'S WHERE IT WENT!

FWIT!

YOU WANT A LICK, RUTHIE?

EEEEEW... WHEN WAS THE LAST TIME YOU WASHED YOUR HAIR?!

YESTERDAY.

OH...OKAY, THEN!

AS AN APOLOGY FOR BREAKING HER PROMISE TO TAKE YOU TO THE OLYMPICS, YOUR GRANDMA MYRNA HAS SENT YOU SOMETHING.

WHAT?!

A GIFT CERTIFICATE.

OH, YES! YIPPEE!!! WHERE IS IT?!

OH.

RUTHIE, DO YOU KNOW WHAT A GIFT CERTIFICATE IS?

NO, AND SO FAR I'M NOT LOVIN' IT.

MOM, I'D LIKE TO SHARE A PERSONAL STORY WITH YOU.

REALLY?

ONCE UPON A TIME, A LITTLE GIRL NAMED GOLDILOCKS...

GOLDILOCKS AND THE THREE BEARS? WHAT MAKES THIS A **PERSONAL** STORY?

GOLDILOCKS HAS A MEAN MOTHER WHO WON'T LET HER WATCH VIDEOS.

RUTHIE, IT'S TOO NICE A DAY TO WATCH TV.

"IT'S TOO NICE A DAY TO WATCH TV," SAID GOLDILOCKS' MOM...

LISTEN, JUST BECAUSE YOU'RE A BIG KID AND A PLAYGROUND SUPERVISOR DOESN'T MAKE YOU KING OF EVERYTHING!

YOU CAN'T BOSS AROUND LITTLE KIDS AND CALL US NAMES... AND I DO NOT LOOK LIKE A SEA MONKEY!

YOU'RE MEAN AND HATEFUL AND YOU'RE NOT A VERY NICE PERSON...

AND ANOTHER THING...

WHY IS IT THAT WHAT I **SHOULD HAVE** SAID IS ALWAYS SO MUCH BETTER THAN WHAT I **DID** SAY?

MOM TOOK MRS. GOULD TO THE DOCTOR'S THIS MORNING.

MRS. GOULD?

YES, SHE HAD A GOPHER REMOVED FROM HER FACE.

YOU MEAN A MOLE?

YES, A MOLE.

MOM, JENNIFER ASKED RUTHIE TO BE IN HER WEDDING, BUT NOT ME.

I KNOW.

SO WHAT SHOULD WE DO ABOUT IT?

WHAT DO YOU **WANT** TO DO ABOUT IT, JOE?

?

SEND JENNIFER A BOX OF FRUIT AND A THANK-YOU NOTE?

GRANDMA AND JENNIFER SURE FIGHT A LOT!

THEY'RE NOT FIGHTS, RUTHIE, THEY'RE SPIRITED DEBATES.

WHAT'S THE DIFFERENCE?

WELL, IN DEBATES, NO PUNCHES ARE THROWN AND THE PARTICIPANTS DON'T RESORT TO NAME-CALLING.

OH, YEAH? JENNIFER CALLED GRANDMA "MENTAL"!

GRANDMOM, YOU ARE SO JUDGMENTAL!

OH, HOW CAN YOU JUDGE ME SO HARSHLY?!

GRANDMOM, YOU **ARE** JUDGMENTAL!

GUILTY!

YOU JUMP RIGHT IN AND **TELL** PEOPLE WHENEVER YOU CATCH THEM DOING SOMETHING ROTTEN OR HARMFUL, AND THAT'S... UH...

AND COME TO THINK OF IT, WHENEVER SOMEBODY DOES SOMETHING **GOOD**, YOU TELL 'EM THAT, TOO... AND I GUESS THAT'S JUDGMENTAL AS WELL...

AND ANOTHER THING, YOU ALWAYS MAKE ME FIGURE OUT THESE THINGS FOR MYSELF!

MORE TEA, DEAR?

TAKE A BATH?! MOM, I JUST **HAD** A BATH YESTERDAY... OR MAYBE IT WAS THE DAY BEFORE.

BUT THAT'S NOT THE POINT! THE POINT IS, I PUT ON CLEAN CLOTHES THIS MORNING!

AND MOST OF THE CLEANNESS FROM THE CLOTHES RUBBED OFF ON ME! BUT DID **THAT** EVER OCCUR TO YOU, HUH?

I GUESS NOT.

MOM SAYS TO WASH YOUR HAIR. YOUR BASEBALL CAP WASN'T FRESH.

COME ON, FRANK, **PLEASE** DO A SONG AT MY WEDDING RECEPTION!

NO! NO! NO!

BUT YOU'RE THE ONLY MEMBER OF THIS ENTIRE FAMILY WITH ANY PERFORMING TALENT!

JENNIFER, **LOOK!** I CAN DO **THIS!**

MNUH! MNUH! MNUH!

THANKS, RUTHIE, BUT COUGHING WITH YOUR MOUTH CLOSED IS NOT WHAT I HAD IN MIND.

I CAN SING LIKE THAT, TOO!

HOW ABOUT, I'M WALKIN' ALONG AND ALL OF A SUDDEN I GRAB MY GUT?

I FALL DOWN. EVERYBODY THINKS I'VE BEEN SHOT, BUT IT'S REALLY POISON.

POISON PUT IN MY DIET SODA BY CLARISSA, MY EVIL TWIN.

NO, RUTHIE, WE WANT YOU TO JUST WALK DOWN THE AISLE AND DROP ROSE PETALS, PLEASE.

I THOUGHT THIS WAS A REHEARSAL!

YES, FOR A WEDDING, NOT MELROSE PLACE.

ONE BIG happy

OKAY, SO HERE'S THE DEAL...

THE BRIDE THROWS AWAY HER FLOWERS AND HER PANTYHOSE AND EVERYBODY GETS ALL EXCITED.

WHEN THEY RUN TO THEIR CAR, EVERYBODY THROWS RICE, AND THAT'S THE ONLY TIME ANYONE'S ALLOWED TO THROW FOOD.

WAIT, WAIT! LET ME START AT THE BEGINNING...

WHEN A MAN AND A LADY ARE IN LOVE AND WANT A LOT OF NICE PRESENTS, THEY HOLD A WEDDING.

THE LADY, "THE BRIDE", MAKES ALL HER GIRL-FRIENDS WEAR UGLY DRESSES THAT ARE HORRIBLE TO LOOK AT.

THE MAN'S "GROOM'S" FRIENDS DRESS LIKE WAITERS AND TELL PEOPLE WHERE TO SIT.

THERE ARE LOTS OF FLOWERS AND EVERYBODY SMELLS GOOD, BUT SOME PEOPLE CRY ANYWAY.

EVERYBODY WALKS DOWN THE AISLE, AND THE BRIDE COMES LAST WITH WHOEVER PAID FOR EVERYTHING.

THEN THE BRIDE AND GROOM AND SOME FRIENDS STAND UP FRONT AND TALK TO A PRIEST OR SOMEBODY. THEN EVERYBODY GOES TO A PARTY.

AT THE PARTY, A LOT OF PEOPLE TALK INTO A MICROPHONE, THEN THE OLD LADIES AND THE LITTLE KIDS DO THE ELECTRIC SLIDE.

WOW, RUTHIE, YOU CERTAINLY HAVE WEDDINGS NAILED.

YEAH, AND I'VE ONLY EVER BEEN TO ONE!

ROSE, WHO ARE YOU TALKING TO?

JOSEPHINE.

JOSEPHINE?! YOU JUST SPENT THE ENTIRE AFTERNOON WITH HER! WHAT MORE COULD YOU POSSIBLY HAVE TO SAY TO EACH OTHER?

HUSH, NICK! NOT EVERYTHING CAN BE DISCUSSED FACE-TO-FACE. CERTAIN THINGS ARE BETTER SAID OVER THE PHONE!

LIKE WHAT?

I'LL CALL YOU LATER AND TELL YOU.

GRANDMA, IF THAT LADY IS BLIND, WHY ARE THE LIGHTS ON IN HER HOUSE?

I MEAN, IF A PERSON CAN'T SEE, SHE'D BE ALL RIGHT IN THE DARK, RIGHT?

RUTHIE, THIS IS TV. IT DOESN'T HAVE TO BE SMART...

IT ONLY HAS TO BE OVER IN AN HOUR.

AND THAT'S ANOTHER THING! HOW DO THEY KNOW MY BEDTIME?!

THE OBJECT OF THE GAME IS TO HIT THE BALL THROUGH THE RINGS, SMASHING IT AGAINST THAT POLE.

POLE, JOE?

OKAY, SO I COULD ONLY FIND ONE OF THESE LI'L POLES!

THINK OF IT THIS WAY, RUTHIE...

SHE HAS YET ANOTHER CAREER!

122

124

ONE BIG HAPPY

Rick DeTorie

A FRIEND IS SOMEONE:

WHO DOESN'T WANT YOU TO GET EATEN.

RUN!

WHO SAVES A PLACE FOR YOU IN LINE.

A FRIEND IS SOMEONE:

WHOSE REFRIGERATOR YOU CAN OPEN WITHOUT ASKING PERMISSION.

WHO, WHEN YOU SHARE A BOTTLE WITH HIM, DOESN'T MAKE A HUGE BIG DEAL OUT OF WIPING OFF THE TOP.

A FRIEND IS SOMEONE:

WHO NEVER HITS YOU.

WHO WATCHES THE SAME TV SHOWS AS YOU EVEN THOUGH HE DOESN'T LIKE THEM.

A FRIEND IS SOMEONE:

WHO, WHEN HE SEES YOU CRY, DOESN'T GO TELL EVERYBODY ABOUT IT.

WHO PROTECTS YOU.

A FRIEND IS SOMEONE:

YOU CAN HANG OUT WITH AND NOT HAVE TO TALK EVERY MINUTE.

WHO HELPS YOU WITH A HOMEWORK ASSIGNMENT LIKE THIS ONE.

TODAY'S MAJOR FEATURE FILMS ARE NOTHING BUT STUNTS AND SPECIAL EFFECTS.

SO YOU AGREE WITH ME THAT TV DRAMA IS NOW SUPERIOR TO FEATURES!

RUTHIE, WHICH DO **YOU** THINK IS BETTER—MOVIES OR TV?

TV.

WHY?

THE BATHROOM'S CLOSER.

WHUMP!

THAT LOOKS VERY PAINFUL!

YEAH, JAMES!

YOU MEANT FOR THE TREE, RIGHT?

OF COURSE.

JAMES, WHY ARE YOU TACKLING TREES?

'CUZ I AIN'T GOT NO FOOTBALL!

AND, YA SEE, WITH FOOTBALL, YA DON'T NEED NO BALL TO TACKLE STUFF! ALL YOU NEED IS THIS HERE!

A BIRD BRAIN?

HUT, HUT!

RUTHIE, THAT WASN'T A NICE THING TO SAY.

SORRY, BIRDS!

THUMP!

126

ONE BIG HAPPY

RICK DETORIE

I HAVE A GREAT SLOGAN FOR YOUR PRESIDENTIAL BID!

SLOGAN? BID?

"VOTE RUTHIE: A SLAVE TO NO ONE AND A SERVANT TO ALL!"

OKAY... SO LONG AS I DON'T HAVE TO MAKE ANYBODY'S BED!

"HOW TO GET TO BE PRESIDENT" BY RUTHIE.

I'M NOT GONNA RUN!

VOTE FOR ME!

FOR A LONG TIME, LIKE TEN YEARS, SOME GUYS TALK ABOUT BEING PRESIDENT.

THEY SAY THEY'RE **RUNNING** FOR PRESIDENT, BUT MOSTLY THEY JUST WALK AND GET OFF PLANES AND STUFF.

HI!

SOME PEOPLE ARE PUBLICANS AND SOME ARE STEMOCRATS, BUT SOME OTHERS RUN, TOO. THEY'RE CALLED UNDEPENDABLES.

HE'S NO GOOD!

HE'S WORSE THAN ME!

THEY BOTH STINK!

THE PRESIDENT GUYS GET TO BE IN A LOT OF COMMERCIALS, BUT NONE OF THEM HAVE ANYTHING USEFUL TO SELL, LIKE ASPIRIN OR PANCAKE SYRUP.

YAK! YAK! YAK!

THEN THERE'S A BIG PARTY WITH LOTS OF BALLOONS, BUT NO CAKE.

YEA! YIP!

YEAH!

WHAT ABOUT TAXES?

WHAT ABOUT GUM CONTROL?

THEN THE MAIN GUYS GET THEIR OWN TV SHOW (IT'S CALLED "DEBATES") WHERE THEY SAY A LOT OF STUFF NOBODY CARES ABOUT.

THEN NORMAL PEOPLE GO TO SCHOOL AND THE POST OFFICE AND SAY WHO SHOULD BE PRESIDENT IN A BOX. THIS IS CALLED AN ELECTION.

BOX

THE WINNER IS ALWAYS WHOEVER HAS THE BEST HAIR. IF YOU GOT **NO** HAIR YOU CAN'T BE PRESIDENT. BALD PRESIDENTS ARE ALL DEAD.

NICE

#1

AND THAT'S THE WHOLE HONEST TRUTH. THANK YOU!